PEGASUS ENCYCLOPEDIA LIBRARY

Chemistry
BASICS OF CHEMISTRY

Edited by: Anil Kumar Tomar & Pallabi B. Tomar
Managing editor: Tapasi De
Designed by: Vijesh Chahal, Anil Kumar and Rohit Kumar
Illustrated by: Suman S. Roy, Tanoy Choudhury
Colouring done by: Vinay Kumar, Sonu, Kiran Kumari & Pradeep Kumar

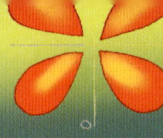

CONTENTS

Introduction 3

Branches of Chemistry 5

What does a chemist do? 8

The International System of Units (SI) 10

Laws of chemical combinations 13

Atomic Theory 18

Orbitals and Quantum Numbers 26

Some famous Nobel Prize winners for Chemistry 30

Test Your Memory 31

Index 32

Introduction

Chemistry is the branch of science in which we study the properties and structure of substances and all the changes they undergo. All substances are made up of matter which exists in three major states – solid, liquid or gas. The constituent particles are held in different ways in these states of matter and they exhibit different characteristic properties. Matter can also be classified into elements, compounds and mixtures. The elements contain particles of only one type which maybe atoms or molecules. The compounds are formed when atoms of two or more elements combine in a fixed ratio to each other while in case of mixtures, there is no fixed ratio of elements. Most of the substances present around us are mixtures.

When the properties of a substance are studied, measurement is inherent. The quantification of these properties requires a system of measurement and units in which the quantities can be expressed. Though many systems of measurement exist, but the scientific community has a uniform and common system throughout the world which is known as International System of Units (abbreviated as SI units). The measurements involve recording of data which are always associated with a certain amount of uncertainty. So, the proper handling of data obtained by measuring the quantities is very important. The uncertainty is taken care of by specifying the number of significant figures in which the observations are reported. The dimensional analysis is useful in expressing the measured quantities in different systems of units. Hence, it is possible to interconvert the

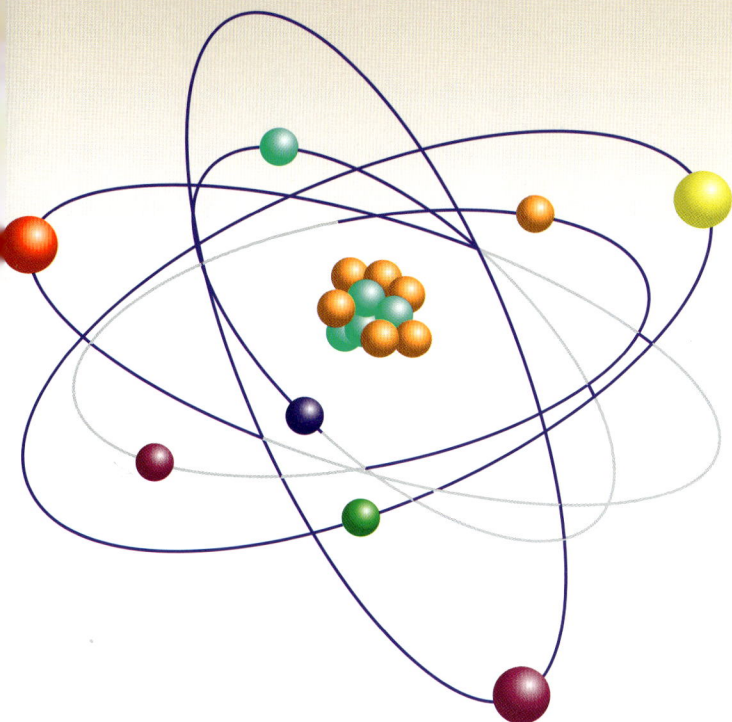

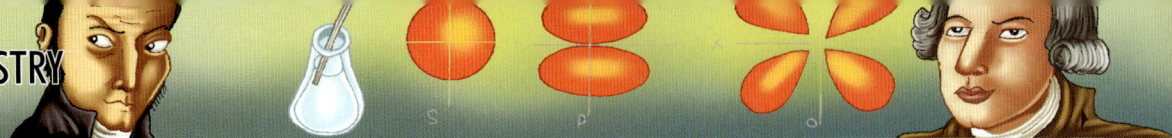

results from one system of units to another.

The combinations of different atoms in molecules and compounds are governed by five basic laws of chemical combination –law of conservation of mass, law of definite proportions, law of multiple proportions, Gay Lussac's law of gaseous volumes and Avogadro law. These laws favour the Dalton's Atomic Theory which states that atoms are building blocks of matter. Atomic mass of an element is most important quantity responsible for chemical properties of an element. Generally, the atomic mass of an element is the average atomic mass obtained by taking into account the natural abundance of different isotopes of that element. The molecular mass of a molecule is calculated by adding the atomic masses of different atoms present in a molecule. The molecular formula can be calculated by determining the mass per cent of different elements present in a compound and its molecular mass. The numbers of atoms, molecules or any other particles present in a system are expressed by Avogadro constant (6.022×10^{23}). This is commonly known as one mole of the respective particles.

The elements and compounds undergo chemical changes which are represented by chemical reactions. A balanced chemical equation provides a lot of information about the nature of a chemical reaction. The coefficients indicate the molar ratios and the respective number of particles taking part in a particular chemical reaction. The stoichiometry is the quantitative study of the reactants required and the products formed. Using various calculations, the amounts of one or more reactant(s) required to produce a definite amount of product can be determined. The amount of particles present in a given volume of a solution can be expressed in number of ways in chemistry, such as mass per cent, mole fraction, molarity and normality.

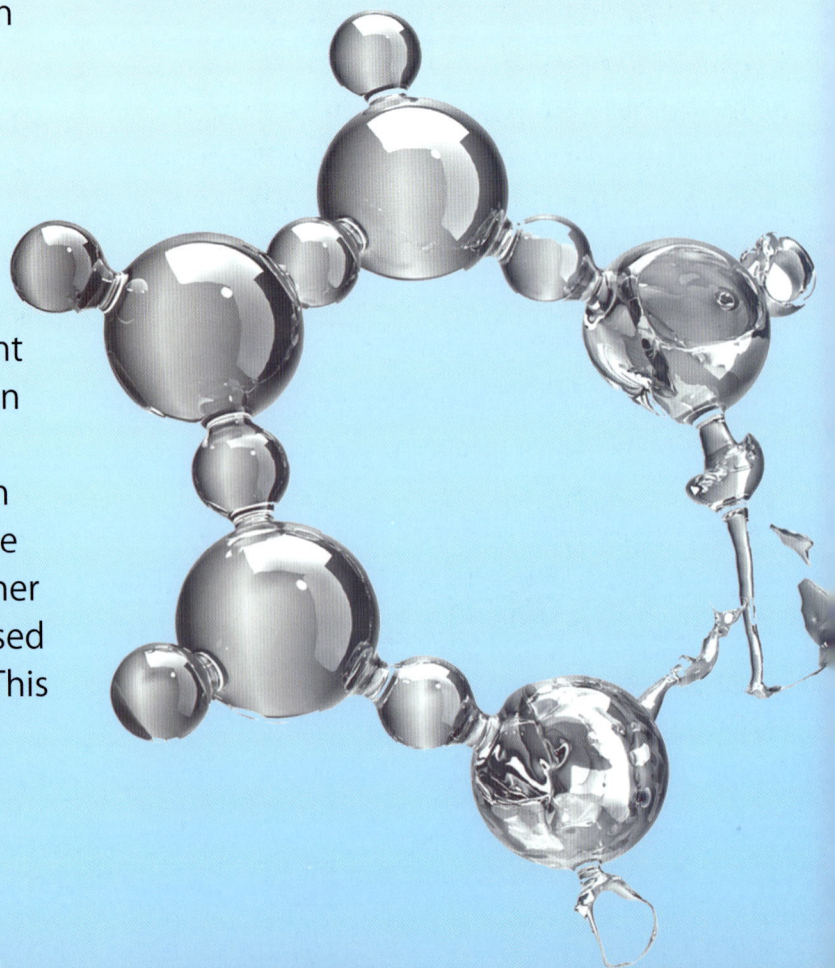

Branches of Chemistry

The field of chemistry is very wide and can be subdivided into a three major areas of specialization— organic, inorganic and physical chemistry.

Organic chemistry

Organic chemistry is the branch of chemistry that deals with the structure, properties and reactions of carbon and its compounds. All living things, both plants and animals, are made out of carbon molecules. Therefore, the molecules which contain carbon are referred as organic molecules. Hydrocarbons are the most common carbon compounds or organic molecules in the Universe. They consist of both carbon and hydrogen in them. The examples of hydrocarbon molecules are carbohydrates, sugars and alcohols etc. The simple hydrocarbon molecules have capabilities of combining together in space to form bigger molecules such as amino acids. As we all know, amino acids are the most important molecules of life because they are the building blocks of enzymes and proteins. The organic molecules make up our hair, skin and fingernails and so on. The diversity of organic chemicals is due to the versatility of the carbon atom to bond with other carbon atoms as well as atoms of other elements.

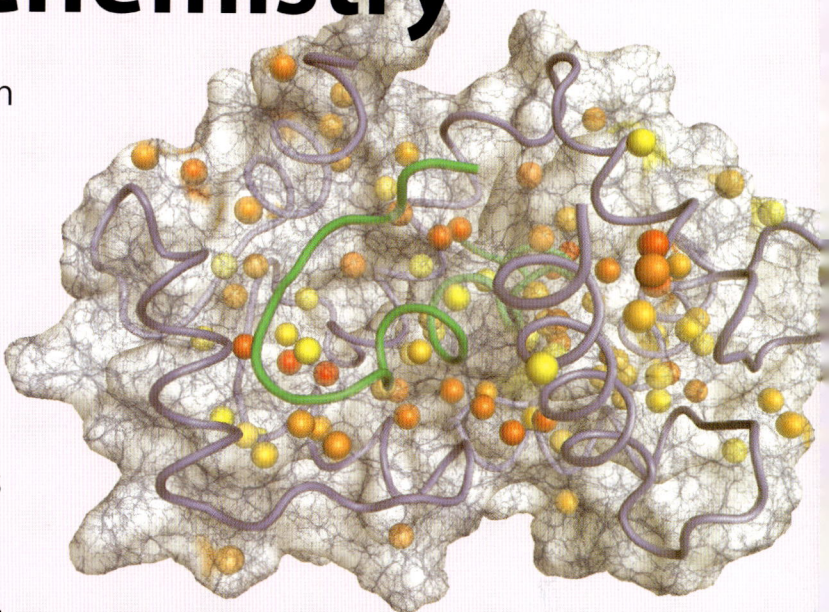

Inorganic chemistry

Inorganic chemistry is the study of the reactions and properties of all the chemical compounds except hydrocarbons. Inorganic chemistry covers an extremely wide range of chemicals and it is classified according to similar groups, periods

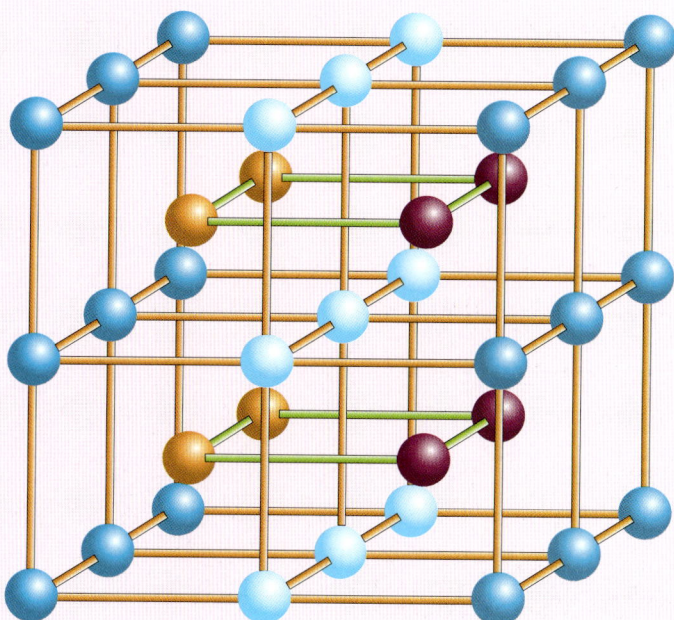

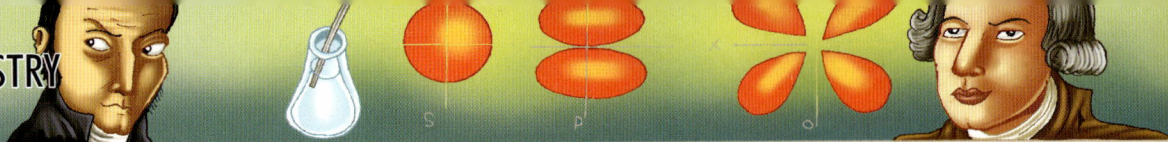

and properties. It covers a broad range of topics, among which are atomic structure, chemical bonding, coordination compounds, acid-base reactions, ceramics and the various subdivisions of electrochemistry (electrolysis, battery science, corrosion, semiconductors, etc.). One important aspect of inorganic elements is the formation of ionic compounds. Ions are charged particles which combine with oppositely charged particles to form compounds. For example: Sodium Chloride (common table salt) and Ammonium Nitrate (a fertilizer).

Physical chemistry

The ways in which organic and inorganic compounds and their constituents react and interact with one another are governed by certain physical laws and principles. Physical chemistry is the branch of chemistry in which we study these laws. So, it is the foundation upon which all other fields of chemistry rest. Physical chemistry is encompassed by three major subject areas, including Thermodynamics, Quantum Chemistry and Chemical Kinetics.

Thermodynamics is the study of the conversion of energy into heat and work. Thermodynamics is also the study of the ways in which the conversion process can be altered by changing variables such as pressure and temperature within a system.

Quantum Chemistry is a theoretical science which describes how molecules bond with one another by applying principles of quantum field theory and quantum mechanics. These principles describe how atoms and subatomic particles behave in various systems and in turn, govern how molecules behave. Theoretically all chemical systems can be described using quantum chemistry, but in practice only very simple systems can be accurately investigated.

Chemical Kinetics studies the rates of chemical processes. The rate of a given chemical process is defined as the speed at which a chemical reaction occurs such that the reactants convert into the product. In chemical kinetics, we also study how changing variables such as pressure and temperature change the rate at which reactions occur.

There are also two other branches of Chemistry— Analytical Chemistry and Biochemistry, which have significant scientific interest of researchers. These are applied fields of chemistry which have evolved a lot in the recent years.

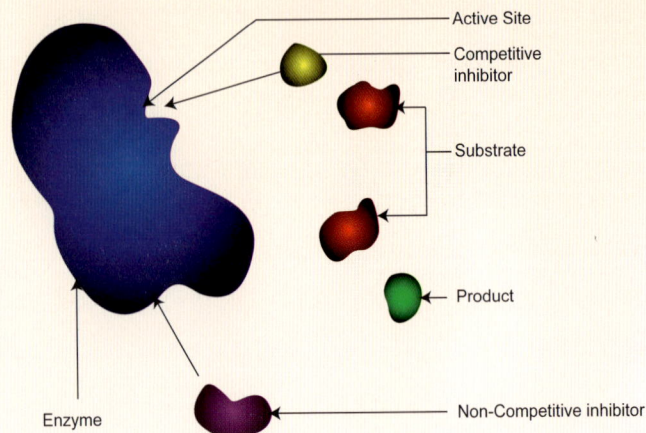

Active Site
Competitive inhibitor
Substrate
Product
Non-Competitive inhibitor
Enzyme

Analytical Chemistry

Analytical Chemistry is the science of obtaining, processing and communicating information about the composition and structure of substances. The identification of a substance, the elucidation of its structure and quantitative analysis of its composition are the main aspects of analytical chemistry. Analytical chemistry has two steps in analysis— characterization and determination of the constituents of a compound. The first step is identification step which is called Qualitative analysis. The second step is about determining the amount of constituents and known as Quantitative analysis. Quantitative analysis can be classified depending upon the method of analysis or according to the scale of analysis.

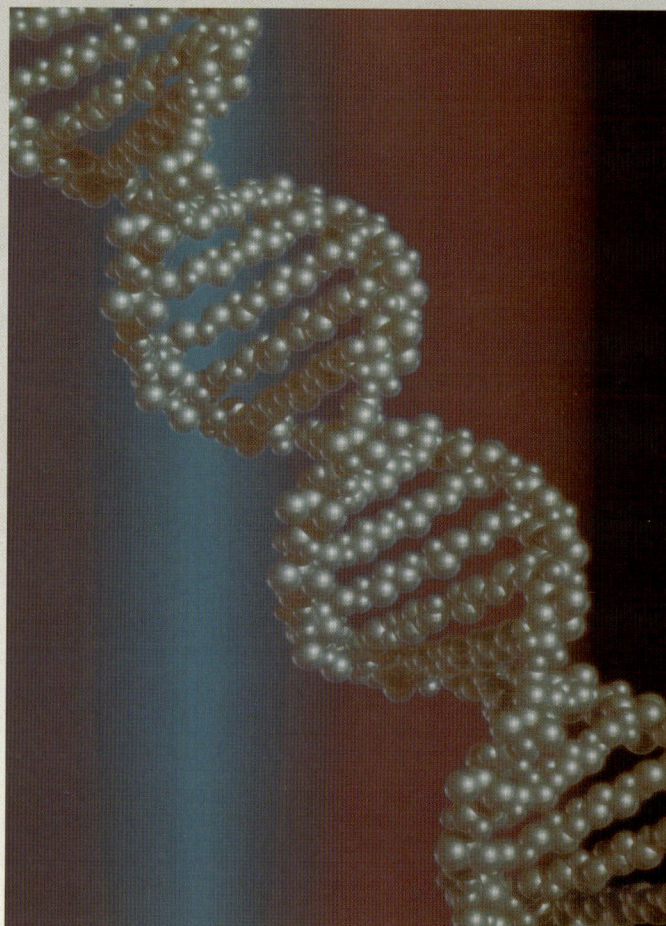

Biochemistry

Biochemistry is the branch of chemistry in which we study about the chemical processes in living organisms. Biochemistry governs all living organisms and living processes. By controlling information flow through biochemical signalling and the flow of chemical energy through metabolism, biochemical processes give rise to the incredible complexity of life. Biochemistry mainly deals with the structural and functional components of cells such as proteins, carbohydrates, lipids, nucleic acids (DNA and RNA) and other biomolecules.

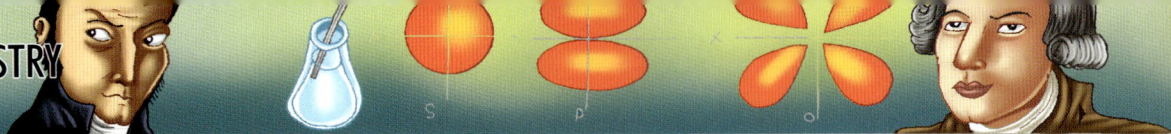

What does a chemist do?

- A chemist is always busy with tedious and very important tasks. A chemist, in his routine work, analyzes substances. He determines the constituent elements of a substance and their amount. He analyzes the substances in all states of matter—solids, liquids and gases. He also searches for the active compounds in a substance. He also does analysis of impurities present in water.

- A chemist also synthesizes new substances. Either he makes the synthetic version of a substance found in nature or he synthesizes an entirely new and unique compound. A chemist creates polymers of elements and compounds for industrial purposes such as plastic and paints. He also tries to find more efficient process to use for the production of an established product.

- A chemist creates models and tests the predictive power of theories. This area of chemistry is referred to as theoretical chemistry. A chemist who works in this branch uses computers to model chemical systems.

- A chemist measures the physical properties of substances. He measures the melting points and boiling points of new compounds and mixtures. He also measures the strength of a new polymer strand.

- A chemist in pharmaceutical company searches for potential drug components and formulates new medicines to cure various diseases.

On the basis of their work, chemists can be classified into various groups. Some important groups are:

Quality control chemists

These chemists analyze raw materials, intermediate products and final products for purity to make sure that they fall within specifications. They may also offer technical support for the customer. Many

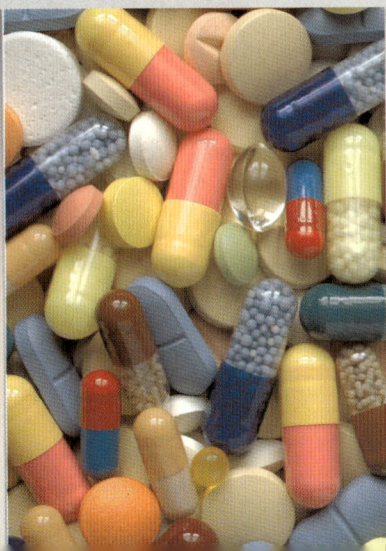

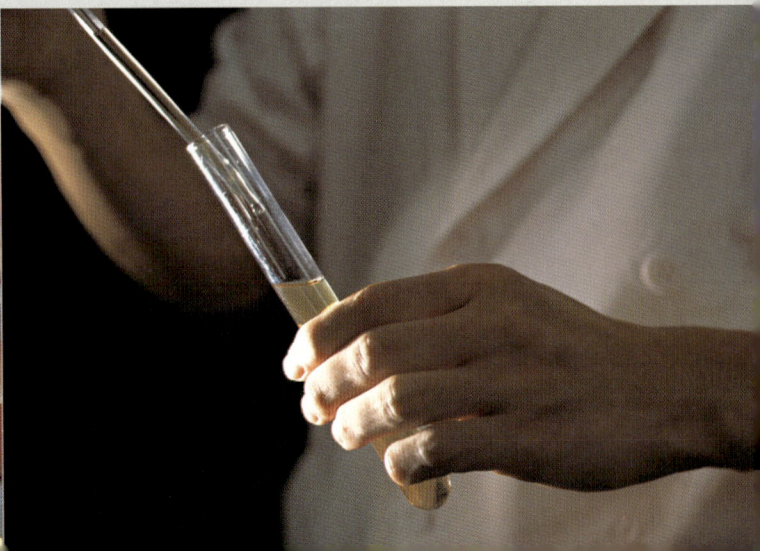

of these chemists often solve problems when they occur within the manufacturing process.

Industrial research chemists

Chemists in this profession perform a large number of physical and chemical tests on materials. They may develop new products, and they may work on improving existing products. They formulate products that meet specific needs.

Sales representatives

Chemists may work as sales representatives for companies that sell chemicals or pharmaceuticals. They reach to the potential customers to advertise new products that are being developed.

Forensic chemists

The forensic chemists analyze samples taken from crime scenes or samples for the presence of drugs.

Environmental chemists

These chemists work for water purification plants, the Environmental Protection Agencies, the Department of Energy or similar agencies. They often go out to sites to collect the samples.

Chemical educators

Chemists also work as educators. They teach physical science and chemistry in schools, colleges and universities. The University chemistry teachers also conduct research work with graduate students.

9

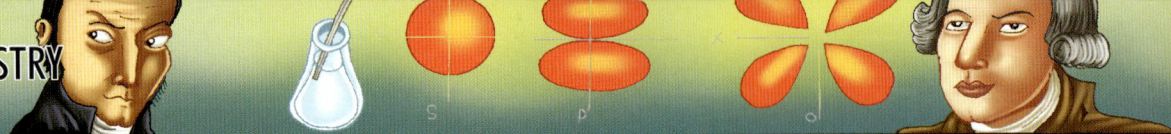

The International System of Units (SI)

The value of a quantity is generally expressed as the product of a number and a unit. The unit is simply a particular example of the quantity concerned which is used as a reference and the number is the ratio of the value of the quantity to the unit. For a particular quantity, we can use many different units. For example, the speed of an object can be expressed as 100 m/s or 360 km/h, where metre per second and kilometre per hour are alternative units for expressing the speed. However, because of the importance of a set of well defined and easily accessible units, the science community universally agreed for the multitude of measurements that support today's complex society. The units should be chosen so that they are readily available to all, are constant throughout time and space and are easy to calculate with high accuracy.

By convention physical quantities are organized in a system of dimensions. All systems of weights and measures, metric and non-metric are linked through a network of international agreements supporting the International System of Units (SI). The SI is maintained by a small agency in Paris, the International Bureau of Weights and Measures. It is updated every few years by an international conference, the General Conference on Weights and Measures. This conference is attended by representatives of all the industrial countries and international scientific and engineering organizations.

SI Base Units

The base quantities used in this system are for length, mass, time, electric current, temperature, amount of substance and

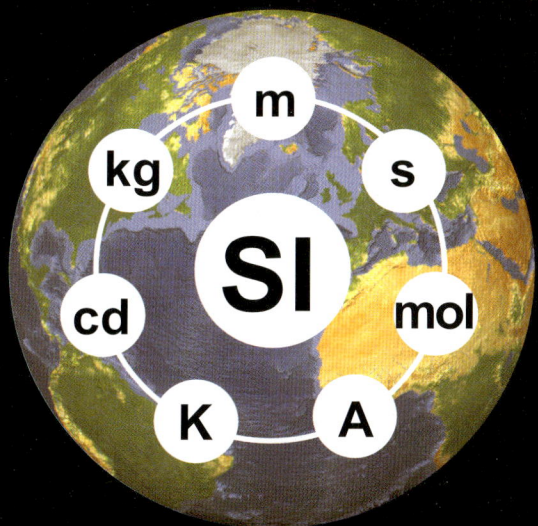

luminous intensity. The base quantities are by convention assumed to be independent.

Each of the seven base quantities used in the SI is regarded as having its own dimension, which is symbolically represented by a single capital letter. The symbols used for the base quantities and the symbols used to denote their dimensions are given as follows:

Base quantity	Symbol for quantity	Symbol for dimension
Length	l, x or r	L
Mass	m	M
Time	t	T
Electric current	I	I
Temperature	T	Θ
Amount of substance	n	N
Luminous intensity	lv	J

The base units are consistent with the part of the metric system called the MKS system. The SI units for seven base quantities are known as base units or fundamental units. Following are the seven base units:

Base quantity	Base unit
Length	metre
Mass	kilogram
Time	second
Electric current	ampere
Temperature	Kelvin
Amount of substance	mole
Luminous intensity	candela

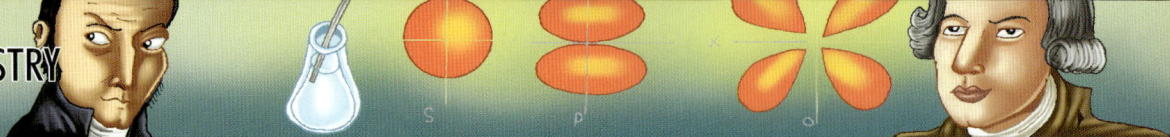

SI Derived Units

All other quantities which are derived from base quantities are called derived quantities. These can be written in terms of the base quantities by the equations of physics. The dimensions of the derived quantities are written as products of powers of the dimensions of the base quantities using the equations. The units for measurement of derived quantities are called derived units. These units are defined algebraically in terms of base units. Currently there are 22 SI derived units. Some important derived units include:

The SI does not allow use of any units other than listed SI base and derived units. In particular, it does not allow use of any of the English traditional units such as horsepower. Also, it does not allow the use of any of the algebraically-derived units of the former CGS system, such as the erg, gauss, poise, stokes and other traditional scientific units such as the torr, curie, calorie or rem.

Quantity	Unit
Plane angle	radian
Force	Newton
Pressure	pascal
Energy	joule
Power	watt
Temperature	degree Celsius
Charge	coulomb
Potential	volt
Capacitance	farad
Resistance	ohm
Luminance	lux
Frequency	hertz
Rates of radioactivity	Becquerel

Laws of chemical combinations

Chemistry deals with the matter and the changes occurring in it; chemists are particularly interested in these changes, where one or more substances are changed into quite different substances. These chemical changes are governed by some empirical laws known as laws of chemical combinations. There are five basic laws of chemical combination of elements to form compounds.

Law of Conservation of Mass

According to law of mass conservation,

the total weight of all the substances taking part in a chemical reaction is same as the total weight of all the substances produced at the end of the reaction. So, in a chemical change, the total weight of the reacting substances is equal to the total weight of the products formed. This law was first formulated by Antoine Lavoisier in 1789. Mikhail Lomonosov, in 1748, had also expressed similar ideas earlier. So, this law is also known as the Lomonosov-Lavoisier law. In its original form, this law states that the mass of substances in a closed system will remain constant, no matter what processes are acting inside the system. So, a matter only changes its form in a chemical reaction but it can neither be created nor destroyed.

For example: 1 gram of hydrogen is found to unite with 8 grams of oxygen to form water. The water produced is found to

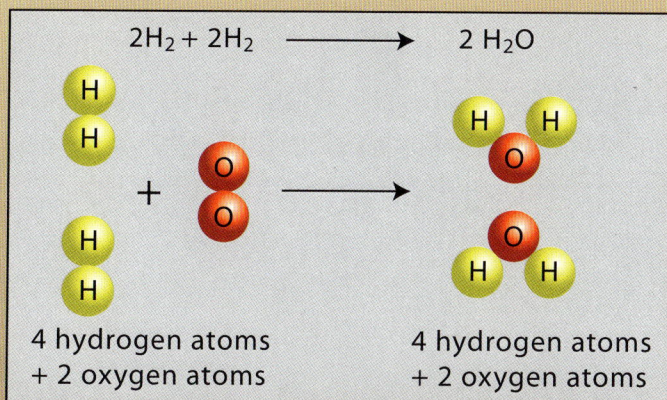

$$2H_2 + 2H_2 \longrightarrow 2 H_2O$$

4 hydrogen atoms + 2 oxygen atoms

4 hydrogen atoms + 2 oxygen atoms

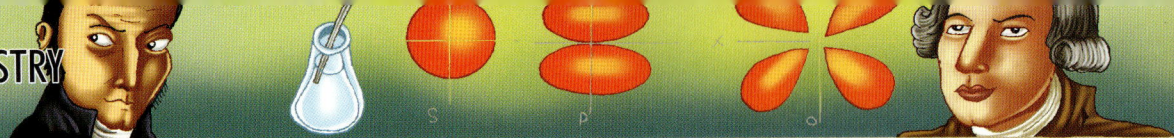

have a weight of nine grams, which is the sum of the weights of the hydrogen and the oxygen.

This law is valid in most of the real cases but in nuclear reactions and in very large astronomical objects, this law becomes questionable.

Law of Definite Proportions

The law of definite proportions was first defined by Joseph Louis Proust. This law states that in a pure compound, the elements combine in definite proportions to one another by mass. This is also known as the law of constant composition. According to this law, a particular chemical compound whatever its method of preparation, always contains the same elements combined in the same proportion by weight.

For example: Carbon dioxide can be prepared either by burning carbon in oxygen or by the action of dilute hydrochloric acid on marble. In both cases, carbon dioxide contains only carbon and oxygen united in the ratio 32 grams of oxygen and 12 grams of carbon. Similarly, water is always composed of two hydrogen atoms and one oxygen atom. In typical preparation it contains about 88.8 per cent oxygen to about 11.2 per cent hydrogen by mass. Hydrogen peroxide is also made up of oxygen and hydrogen but with a different proportion of hydrogen to oxygen than water.

There is one class of substances called non-stoichiometric compounds or Berthollides that are an exception to this law. The ratio between elements in these compounds can vary within certain limits.

For example: Rust or ferrous oxide its primary formula is simply FeO but the amount of iron and oxygen can vary significantly at different places.

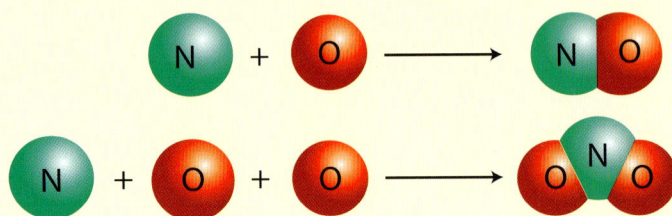

Law of Multiple Proportions

The multiple proportions bring out the relationship between the different weights of one of the elements which combine with a fixed weight of the other element to form the different compounds. The law of multiple proportions states that,

"If two elements combine and form more than one compound, the different weights of one of the elements which combine with a fixed weight of the other to form the different compounds are in the ratio of small integers."

For example: Hydrogen and oxygen form two compounds water and hydrogen peroxide. In water and hydrogen peroxide, 1 gram of hydrogen unites with 8 grams of oxygen and 16 grams of oxygen respectively. The different weights of oxygen combining with 1 gram of hydrogen in these two compounds are respectively 8 and 16. So, oxygen weights are in the ratio 1:2 which is a simple ratio. Similarly, oxygen in CO and CO_2 also has a simple 1:2 ratio.

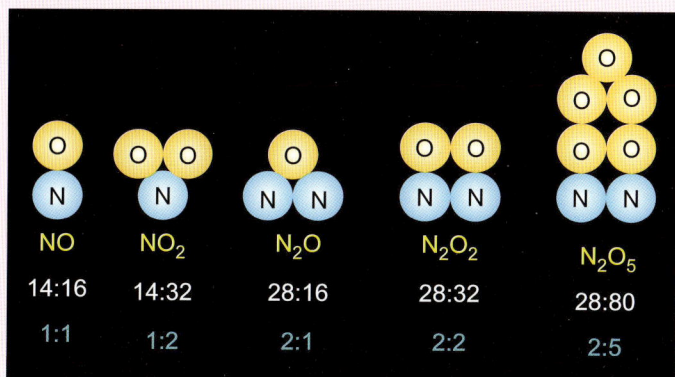

NO	NO_2	N_2O	N_2O_2	N_2O_5
14:16	14:32	28:16	28:32	28:80
1:1	1:2	2:1	2:2	2:5

This law was composed by John Dalton based on the law of definite proportions. This law was the basis of his atomic theory and chemical formulas for compounds. Though the proportions can get quite complex, as with large hydrocarbon molecules, it holds true with great accuracy.

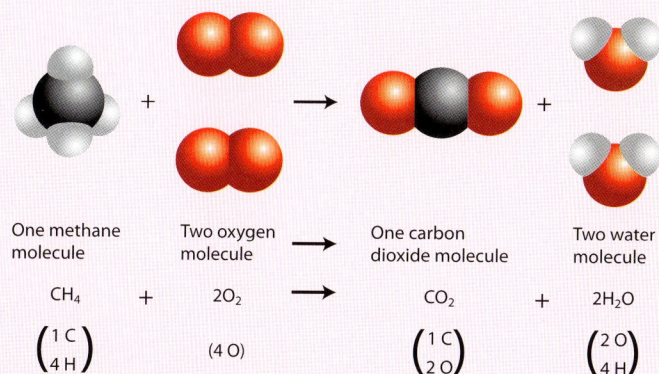

One methane molecule	Two oxygen molecules		One carbon dioxide molecule	Two water molecule
CH_4	+	$2O_2$ →	CO_2	+	$2H_2O$
$\binom{1\,C}{4\,H}$		(4 O)	$\binom{1\,C}{2\,O}$	$\binom{2\,O}{4\,H}$

The law of Reciprocal Proportions

The Law of Reciprocal Proportions was expressed by Ritcher in 1792-94. This law states that, "When two different elements separately combine with the fixed mass of third element, the proportion in which they combine with one another shall be either in the same ratio or some simple multiple of it". This is also known as the law of equivalent proportions.

For example: Sodium and hydrogen unite and form the compound sodium hydride in the ratio 23:1 by weight. Sodium and chlorine form sodium chloride by uniting in the ratio 23:35.5. So, the weights of hydrogen and chlorine which unite with identical weights of sodium are 1 and 35.5 respectively. According to the law of reciprocal proportion, when hydrogen and chlorine combine they should always combine in the ratio 1:35.5 or simple multiple of it.

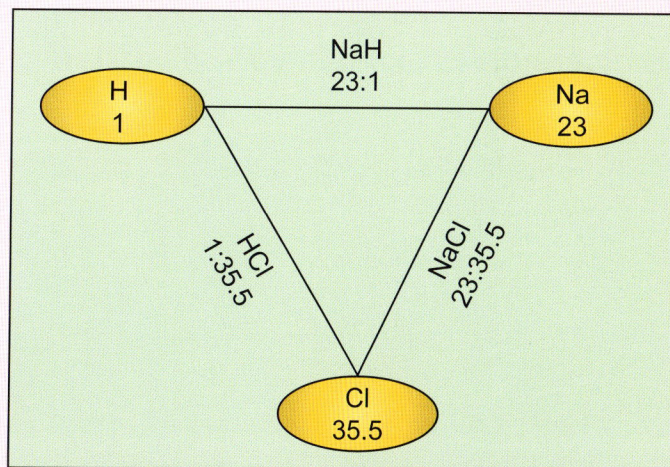

Another **example** can be illustrated as: Two elements C and O separately combine with H to form methane (CH_4) and water (H_2O) respectively. It is very clear that in

15

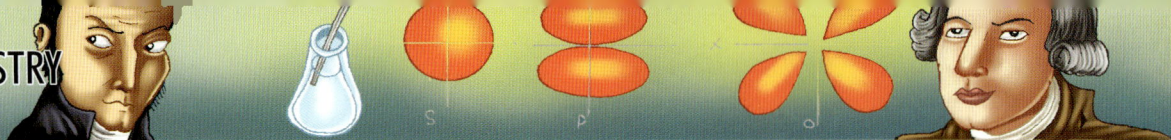

methane 3g of C with 1g of hydrogen, and in water 8g of O with the same mass of H. The ratio of C and oxygen to combine with hydrogen will be 3:8. So, when C and O combine with each other to form carbon dioxide (CO_2), they do so in the same proportion (such that, $12:32 = 3:8$).

Gay Lussac's Law of Gaseous Volumes

The law of gaseous volumes was discovered by Gay Lussac. This law states that when gases combine chemically they do so in volumes which bear a simple ratio to one another. If the product is also gaseous, its volume also bears a simple ratio to the volumes of the interacting gases. An important requirement is that volumes of all the gases should be measured under the same conditions of temperature and pressure.

Some examples of this law are illustrated as the following:

1. Two litres of nitrogen gas reacts with 3 litres of hydrogen gas to produce 2 litres of ammonia gas.

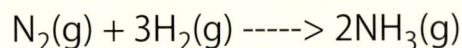

$$N_2(g) + 3H_2(g) \text{-----}> 2NH_3(g)$$

Since all the reactants and products are gases, the mole ratio of $N_2(g):H_2(g):NH_3(g)$ of 1:3:2 is a simple ratio.

2. Two litres of hydrogen gas react with 1 litre of oxygen gas to produce 2 litres of water vapour.

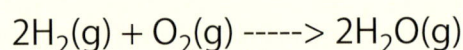

$$2H_2(g) + O_2(g) \text{-----}> 2H_2O(g)$$

Since all the reactants and products are gases, the mole ratio of $H_2(g):O_2(g):H_2O(g)$ of 2:1:2 is a simple ratio of the volumes of gases.

When liquid water undergoes electrolysis to produce hydrogen gas and oxygen gas, the volumes of hydrogen gas and oxygen gas are produced in the ratio of 2:1 but the volume of liquid water required does not follow this relationship since the liquid water is not a gas.

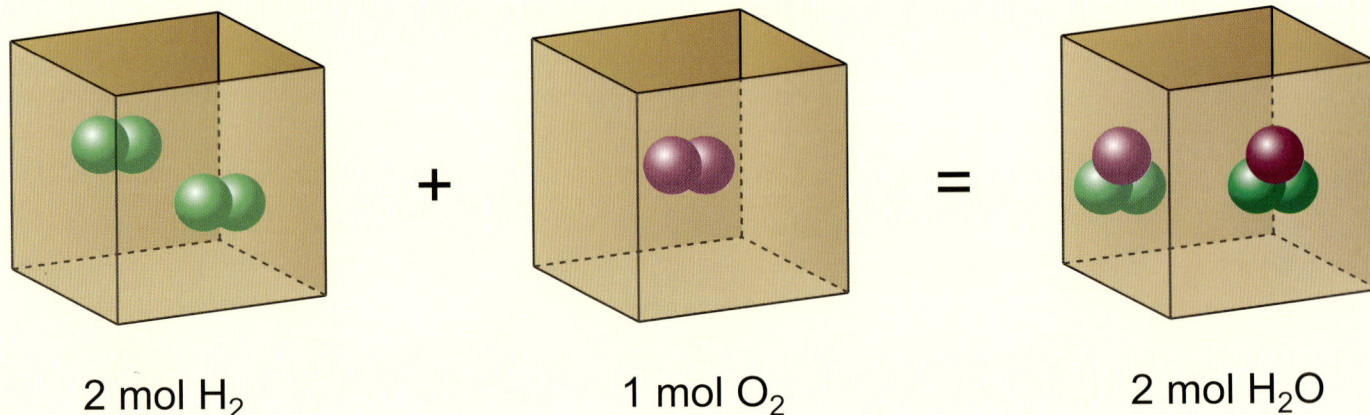

2 mol H_2 +   1 mol O_2 =   2 mol H_2O

Avogadro Law

Avogadro's law is a principle formulated in 1811 by the Italian chemist Amedeo Avogadro. This law states that, **"Equal volumes of gases at the same temperature and pressure contain the same number of molecules regardless of their chemical nature and physical properties"**. This number is known as Avogadro's number and is equal to 6.022 X 10^{23}. It is the number of molecules of any gas present in a volume of 22.4 L. This number is the same for the lightest gas hydrogen as well as for a heavy gas such as carbon dioxide or bromine.

The law can be stated mathematically,

V/n = constant

Where, V is the volume of the gas and n is the amount of substance of the gas.

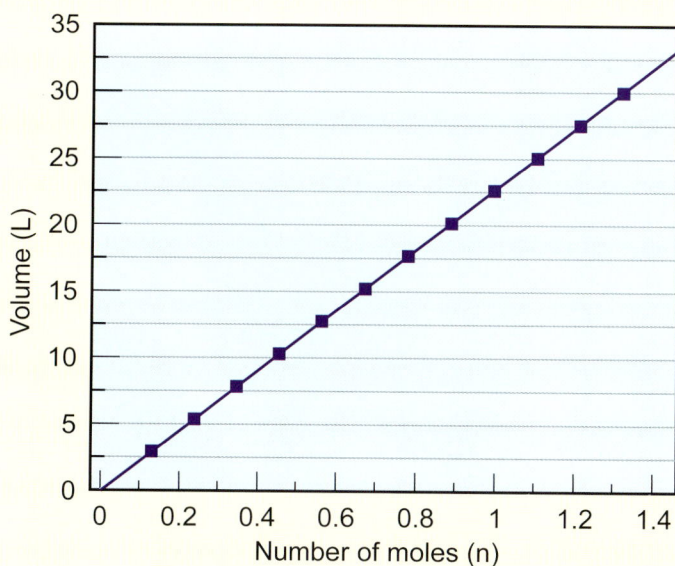

Avogadro's number is one of the fundamental constants of chemistry. It is conventionally represented by 'N' in chemical calculations and is considered to be the number of atoms present in 12 grams of the carbon-12 isotope and can be applied to any type of chemical entity.

It permits calculation of the amount of pure substance (mole), the basis of stoichiometric relationships. It also makes possible to determine how much heavier a simple molecule of one gas is than that of another. So, the relative molecular weights of gases can be ascertained by comparing the weights of equal volumes.

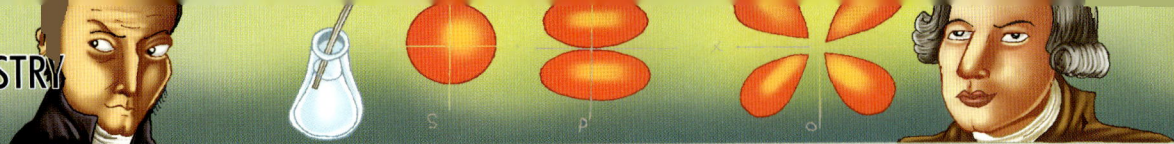

Atomic Theory

Atomic theory is one of the greatest scientific discoveries of the 19th Century which marks the beginning of modern chemistry. A British school teacher, John Dalton, formulated this theory in the year 1803. Though the earliest atomic theories were proposed by Democritus and Aristotle, the first accepted theory was proposed by John Dalton. For the first time in history, he recognized the difference between atom and compounds. This theory is based on his experiments and laws of chemical combinations.

Main postulates of Dalton's atomic theory are:

1. All matter is made of indivisible and indestructible particles called atoms.

2. All atoms of the same element are identical in mass and properties but they differ from the atoms of other elements.

3. Compounds are formed by a combination of atoms of two or more elements in a fixed whole number ratio.

4. Atoms are the smallest unit of matter and a chemical reaction is a rearrangement of atoms.

Though this theory had many drawbacks and its assumptions were proved wrong but it enabled us to explain the laws of chemical combination.

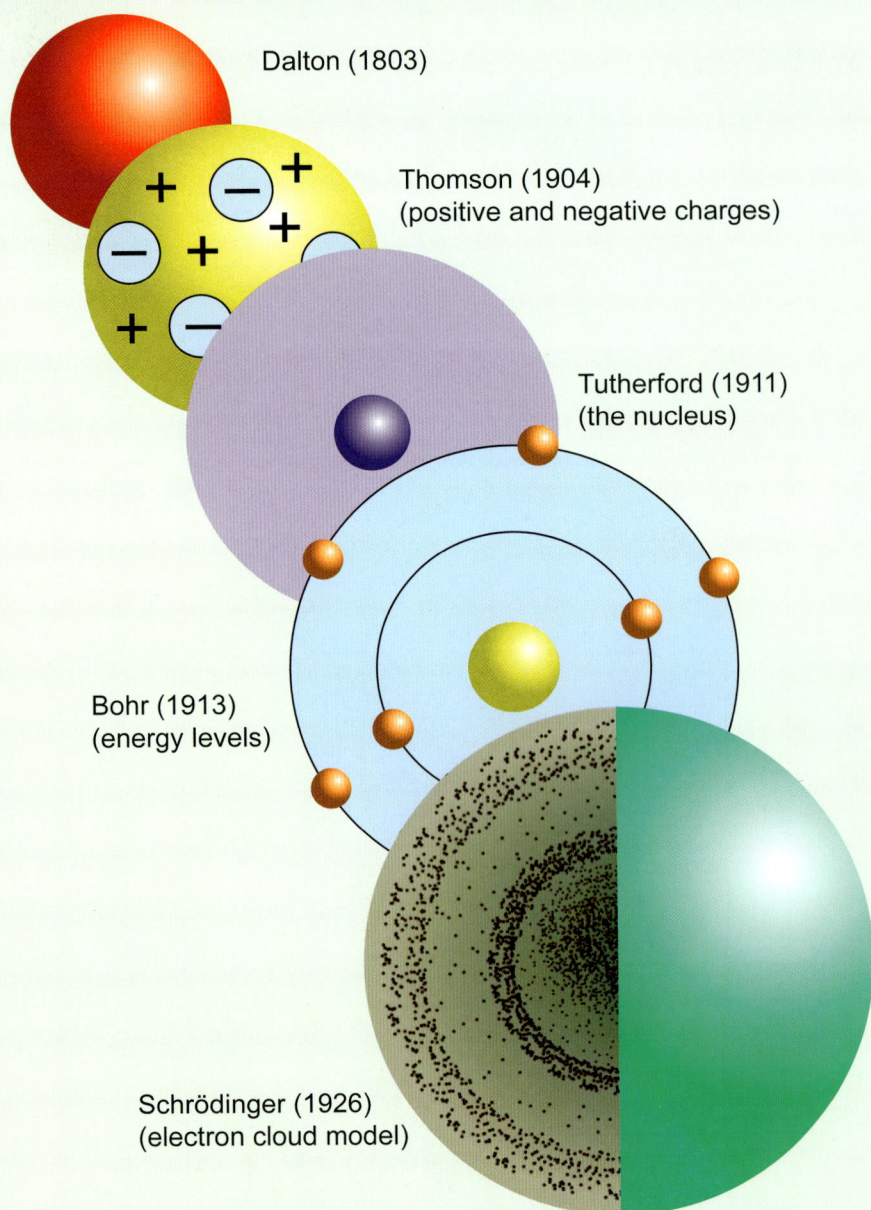

Dalton (1803)

Thomson (1904)
(positive and negative charges)

Tutherford (1911)
(the nucleus)

Bohr (1913)
(energy levels)

Schrödinger (1926)
(electron cloud model)

18

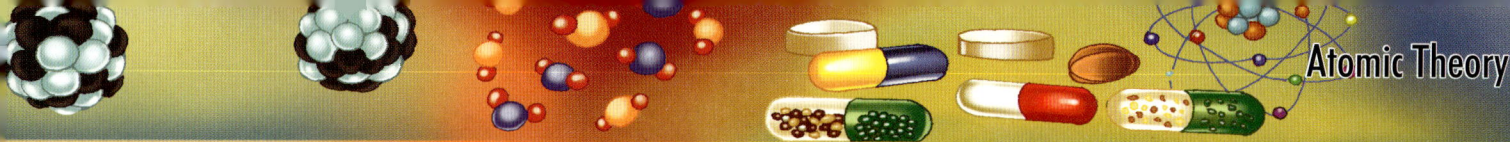

In 1808, John Dalton published a list of elements along with their atomic weights in his 'New System of Chemical Philosophy', for which he received the Royal Medal in 1826. He referred the masses of elements as weights. Since then, chemists used either 'atomic weight' or 'atomic mass'. In spite of the fact that there are some flaws in his work, John Dalton was the pioneer who had given a path breaking view to future experimentations.

Atom and subatomic particles

Atoms are the smallest size pieces that elements come in. Two or more atoms combine together to form a molecule.

Some molecules have atoms of just one type while others may have different types of atoms. For example, an oxygen molecule (O_2) has two oxygen atoms and methane (CH_4) has one carbon atom and four hydrogen atoms.

Atoms are made up of three particles—electron, proton and neutron. Hydrogen atom is an exception as it does not have any neutron. The nucleus of an atom makes up the most of an atom's mass and consists of protons and neutrons. The electrons are smaller particles and revolve around the nucleus. The protons and electrons have positive and negative charges respectively while the neutrons are electrically neutral. An atom has the same number of electrons and protons to make it electrically neutral.

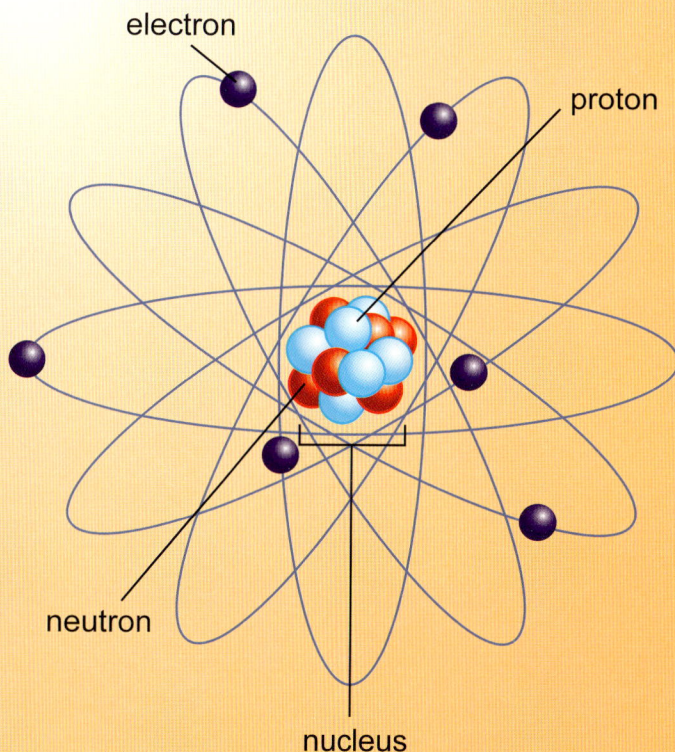

electron

proton

neutron

nucleus

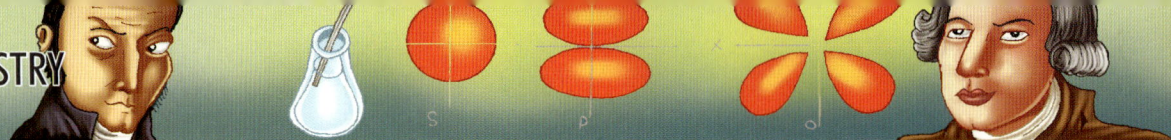

The Electron

Dalton's atomic theory stated that atoms make up all matter in the universe and they were, by definition, indivisible. But even before the entire scientific community accepted the facts of this theory, scientists disapproved the fact that atoms are indivisible. They believed that atoms were made up of even smaller entities.

In 1897, the British Physicist J.J. Thompson discovered the first subatomic particle – the electron while he was experimenting with a cathode ray tube at Cambridge University. He was working to find the constituent particles of cathode rays. In his experiment, he was able to bend the ray using a magnetic field and measured the direction in which the ray bent to determine both mass and charge. Based on his experiments, he proposed that something smaller than an atom existed in the form of tiny negatively charged particles.

Now it is well established that electrons are fundamental aspects of the atomic structure and they provide necessary charge to neutralize the atomic structure. The molecules are formed by combinations of atoms and these combinations are only possible by the bonds formed by electrons. An electron has a mass of 9.11×10^{-31} kg and a charge equal to 1.602×10^{-19} coulomb.

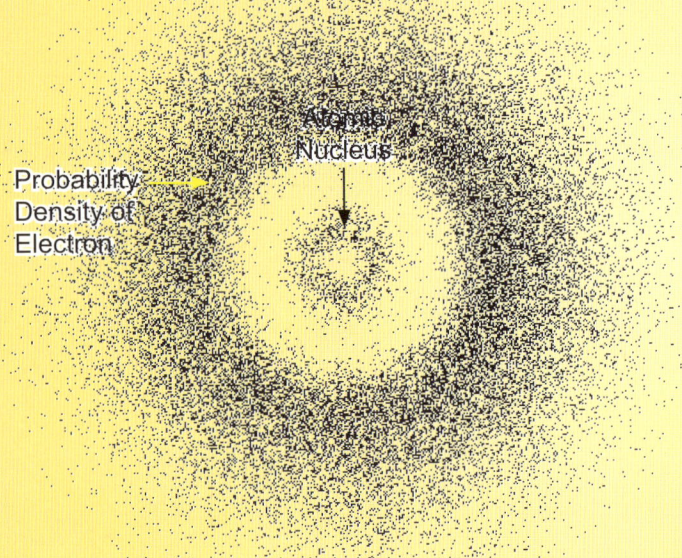

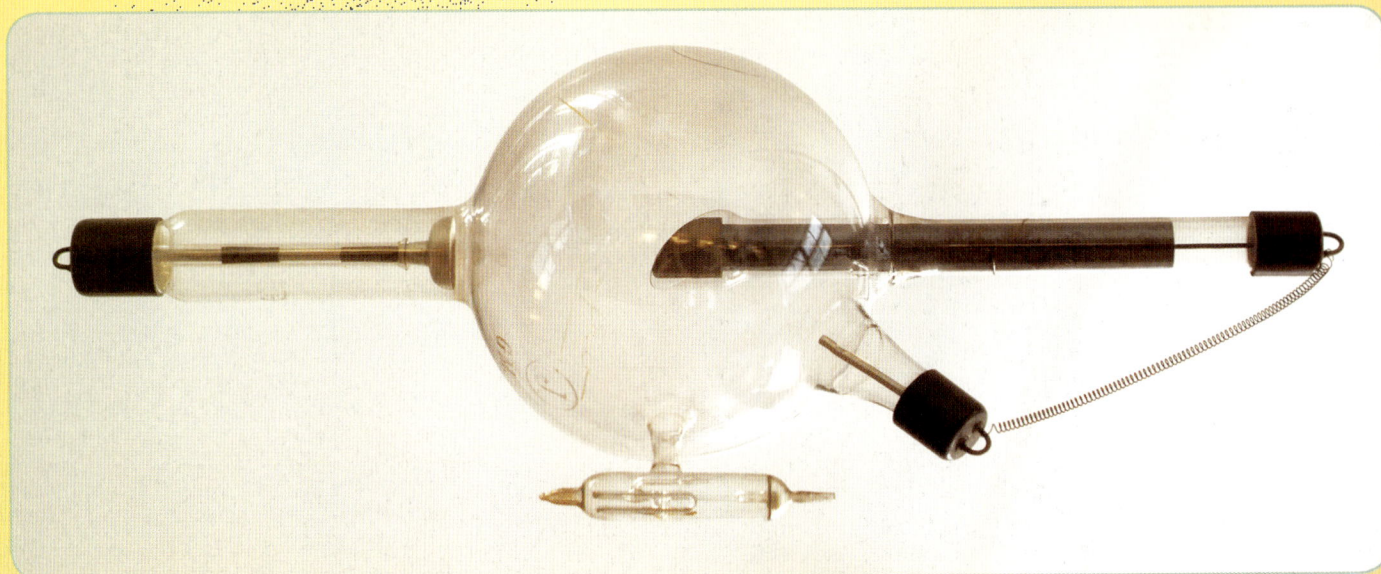

Atomic Nucleus

Probability Density of Electron

The Nucleus

The positively charged nucleus of an atom was discovered by New Zealand physicist Ernest Rutherford in 1909 during the Gold Foil experiment. This experiment was performed by Hans Geiger and Ernest Marsden at the University of Manchester under his guidance. In this experiment, positively charged alpha particles were fired at a high velocity into a very thin sheet of gold foil. The trajectories of these particles after passing through the foil were then detected and analyzed. Most of the alpha particles travelled straight through the foil with little or no deviation and a small fraction rebounded, ending up on the same side of the foil as the incoming beam. Based on these observations, Rutherford proposed new atomic model which states that the negatively charged electrons orbited around a positively charged and incredibly dense central 'nucleus'. Through a series of experiments in 1918, Rutherford discovered the positively charged particles known as the proton. He also deduced that they are subatomic particles and the atom is divisible. The mass of a proton is 1.6726×10^{-27} kg and a charge equal to 1.602×10^{-19} coulomb.

The Neutron

The neutron was discovered by James Chadwick in 1932. He bombarded beryllium (Be) with alpha particles and allowed the radiation emitted by beryllium to incident on a paraffin wax. It was found that protons were scattered out from the paraffin wax. He analyzed the scattered data and proved that the radiation consisted of neutral particles of mass approximately equal to that of proton. These neutral particles were named neutrons. Sir Chadwick was awarded with Noble Prize of Physics for his findings in 1935.

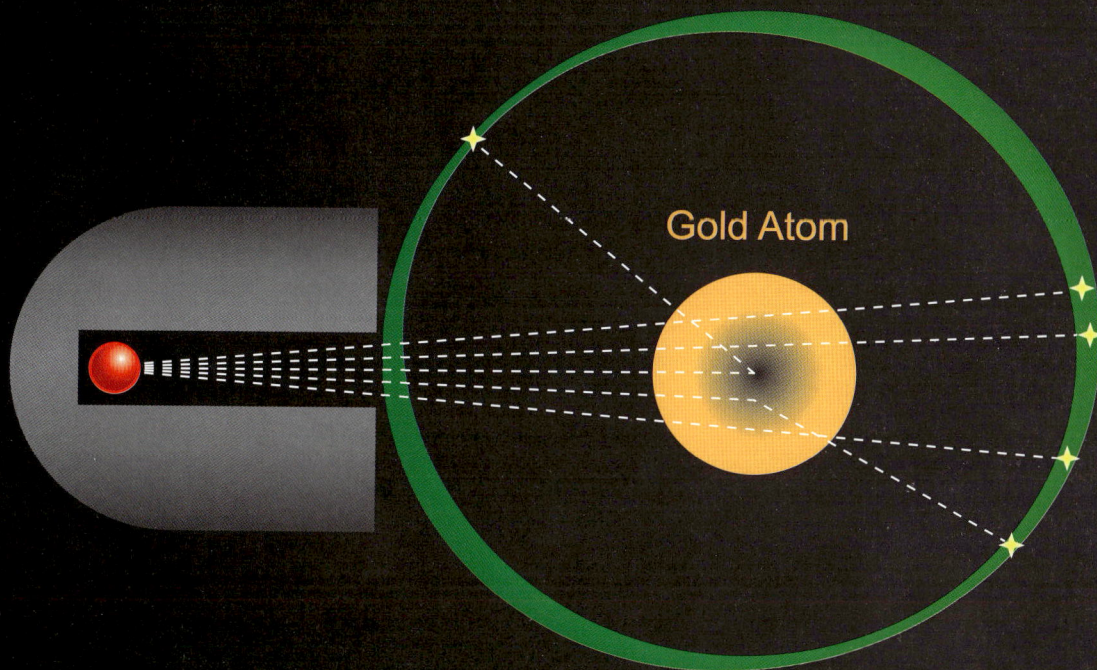

Gold Atom

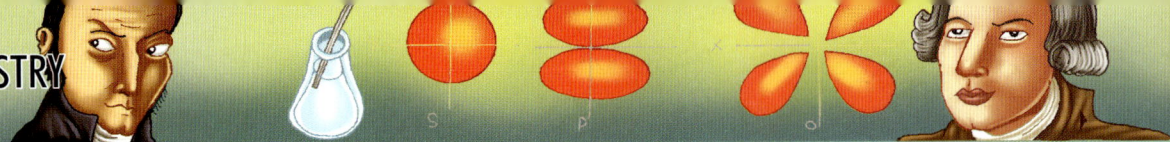

The discoveries of electrons, protons and neutrons marked the adoption of the Rutherford-Bohr model of the atom. The main assumptions of this model are:

- The nucleus of an atom is made up of protons and neutrons which are bound together by strong nuclear forces.

- Electrons orbit the nucleus in the fixed shells.

- Electrons and protons carry equal but opposite charges. The number of electrons and protons is the same in a neutral atom.

Molecules

Molecules are made from atoms of one or more elements. The atoms in a molecule are held together because they share or exchange electrons. Most things around us are molecules made of groups of atoms bonded together. Some molecules contain single type of atoms, such as nitrogen molecule (N2) and some are made up of two or more types of atoms such as, water (H2O). There is a large range of molecules. Some are very small in size containing only few atoms, such as water, carbon dioxide etc. Some molecules have large number of atoms and known as macromolecules, for example, proteins.

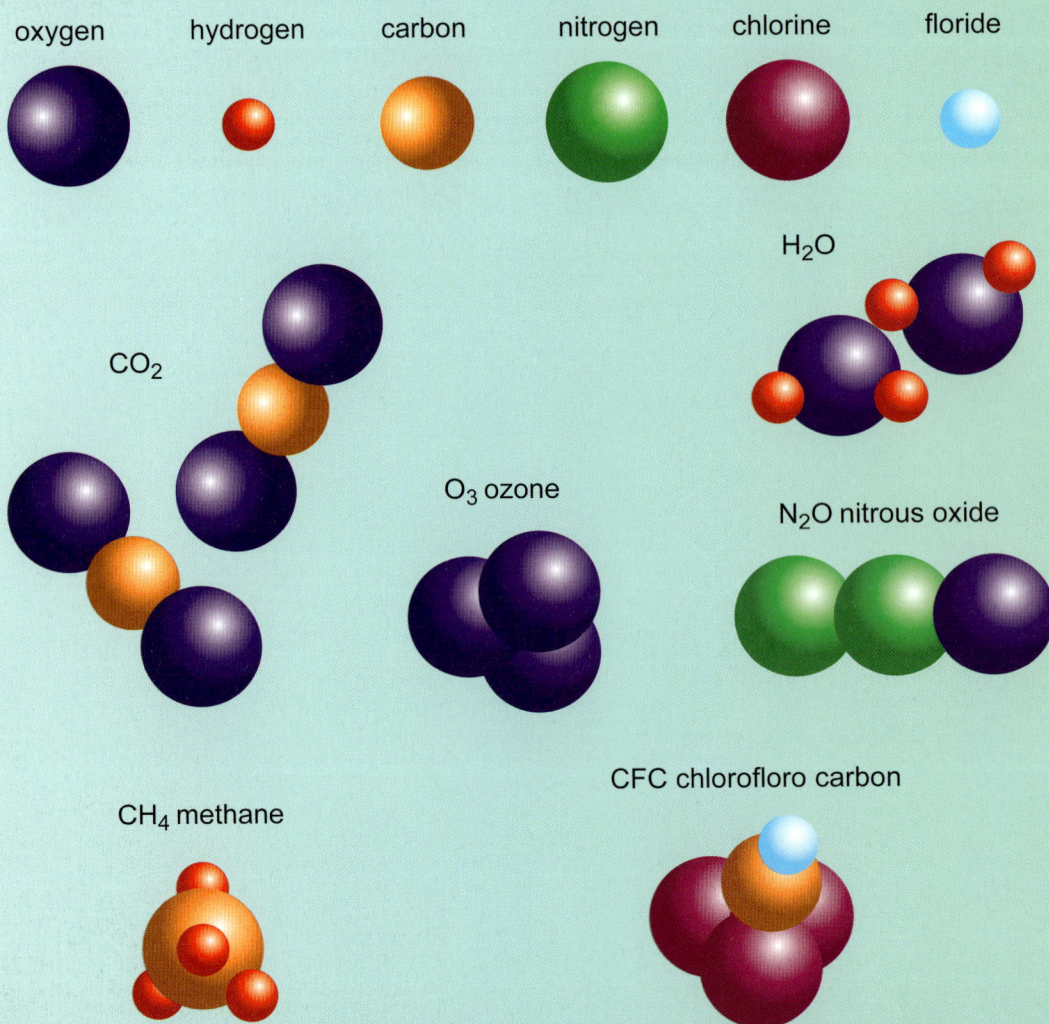

oxygen   hydrogen   carbon   nitrogen   chlorine   floride

CO_2

H_2O

O_3 ozone

N_2O nitrous oxide

CFC chlorofloro carbon

CH_4 methane

Atomic mass

We know that the size of something is measured by its mass. Scientists can even measure very tiny particles like atoms. The size of an atom is measured as its atomic mass. Almost all of the mass of an atom is in its nucleus, so atomic mass can be assumed as a measure of the size of the nucleus of an atom.

The nucleus of an atom is made up of protons and neutrons. Protons and neutrons are almost exactly the same size. The number of protons in the nucleus of an atom is called **atomic number**. The sum of the number of protons and neutrons in the nucleus of an atom is known as **atomic mass**. For example, a hydrogen atom has just one proton and zero neutrons, so its atomic mass is 1. Carbon atom has 6 neutrons and 6 protons, so its atomic mass is 12. Scientists generally use the letter 'Z' to stand for atomic number and the letter 'A' to stand for atomic mass.

Molecular mass

In theory, the relative molecular mass or molecular weight of a compound is the mass of a molecule of the compound relative to the mass of a carbon atom taken as exactly 12. In practice, the molecular mass or molecular weight of a compound is the sum of the atomic masses of the atomic species as given in the molecular formula.

For example, carbon monoxide (CO) is composed of one atom of carbon and one atom of oxygen. Atomic masses of carbon and oxygen are 12.01 and 16.00 respectively. So, molecular mass of CO will be 12.01 + 16.00 = 28.01.

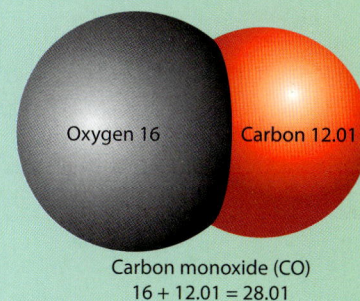

Oxygen 16   Carbon 12.01

Carbon monoxide (CO)
16 + 12.01 = 28.01

1																	2
H																	He
3	4											5	6	7	8	9	10
Li	Be											B	C	N	O	F	Ne
11	12											13	14	15	16	17	18
Na	Mg											Al	Si	P	S	Cl	Ar
19	20	21	22	23	24	25	26	27	28	29	30	31	32	33	34	35	36
K	Ca	Sc	Ti	V	Cr	Mn	Fe	Co	Ni	Cu	Zn	Ga	Ge	As	Se	Br	Kr
37	38	39	40	41	42	43	44	45	46	47	48	49	50	51	52	53	54
Rb	Sr	Y	Zr	Nb	Mo	Tc	Ru	Rh	Pd	Ag	Cd	In	Sn	Sb	Te	I	Xe
55	56	57	72	73	74	75	76	77	78	79	80	81	82	83	84	85	86
Cs	Ba	[1]La	Hf	Ta	W	Re	Os	Ir	Pt	Au	Hg	Tl	Pb	Bi	Po	At	Rn
87	88	89	104	105													
Fr	Ra	[2]Ac	Rf	Db													

[1] Lanthanide	58	59	60	61	62	63	64	65	66	67	68	69	70	71
	Ce	Pr	Nd	Pm	Sm	Eu	Gd	Tb	Dy	Ho	Er	Tm	Yb	Lu
[2] Actinide series	90	91	92	93	94	95	96	97	98	99	100	101	102	103
	Th	Pa	U	Np	Pu	Am	Cm	Bk	Cf	Es	Fm	Md	No	Lr

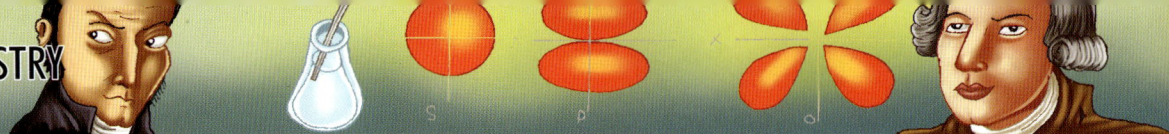

Empirical formula

The percentage composition of a compound leads directly to its empirical formula. An empirical formula for a compound is the formula of a substance written with the lowest integer subscripts. It can be calculated from the per cent composition of a compound. The molecular formula tells us the precise number of atoms of different elements in the substance. The empirical number tells us ratio of numbers of atoms in the compound. The empirical formula of hydrogen peroxide is HO and its molecular formula is H_2O_2. Compounds with different molecular formulas can have the same empirical formulas and such substances will have the same percentage composition of different elements.

For example, acetylene (C_2H_2) and benzene (C_6H_6); in order to obtain the molecular formula of a substance, we need to know the per cent composition and the molecular weight of its components. The molecular weight helps us to choose the correct multiple of the empirical formula to get the molecular formula.

The empirical formula mass of a compound refers to the sum of the atomic masses of the elements present in the empirical formula.

The molecular weight of a compound is a multiple of the empirical formula mass.

Molecular weight = n x empirical formula mass

Empirical formula

A molecule is made up of 79.85 per cent Carbon and 20.15 per cent Hydrogen

Step 1: For 100 gram sample, there will be 79.85 g carbon and 0.15g hydrogen. Now, convert both into moles

79.85g C $\rightarrow$ 6.65 mole carbon; 20.15g H $\rightarrow$ 19.95 mole hydrogen

Step 2: Convert both into moles

79.85g C $\rightarrow$ 6.65 mole carbon; 20.14g H $\rightarrow$ 19.95 mole hydrogen

Step 3: Divide all mole values by the lowest

6.65 mol C/6.65 = 1 mol C; 19.95 mol H/6.65 = 3 mol H

The ratio is 1/# $\rightarrow$ CH_3 is the empirical formula

Isotopes, isobars and isotones

Isotopes are the elements having same atomic number but different mass number. They have the same atomic number because the number of protons inside their nuclei remains the same. The difference in their mass number is due to the difference in their number of neutrons.

Since isotopes have the same number of electrons, they are neutral elements, which make them to possess identical chemical properties. The isotopes can either occur naturally or can be produced artificially in the laboratory.

For example, $_1H^1$, $_1H^2$, $_1H^3$ are all isotopes of hydrogen. They all have their atomic number to be unity but the number of neutrons varies as 0, 1 and 2 respectively. Similarly, $_{17}Cl^{37}$ and $_{17}Cl^{35}$ are isotopes of chlorine.

Isobars are elements, which are chemically different but physically same. They are atoms of different elements having the same atomic mass but different atomic number. Since their number of electrons is different, their chemical properties are different. The light nuclei have unstable isobars while heavy nuclei have stable isobars.

Isotones are elements which have the same number of neutrons. For examples, Chlorine-37 and Potassium-39 are isotones as both have 20 neutrons in their nuclei.

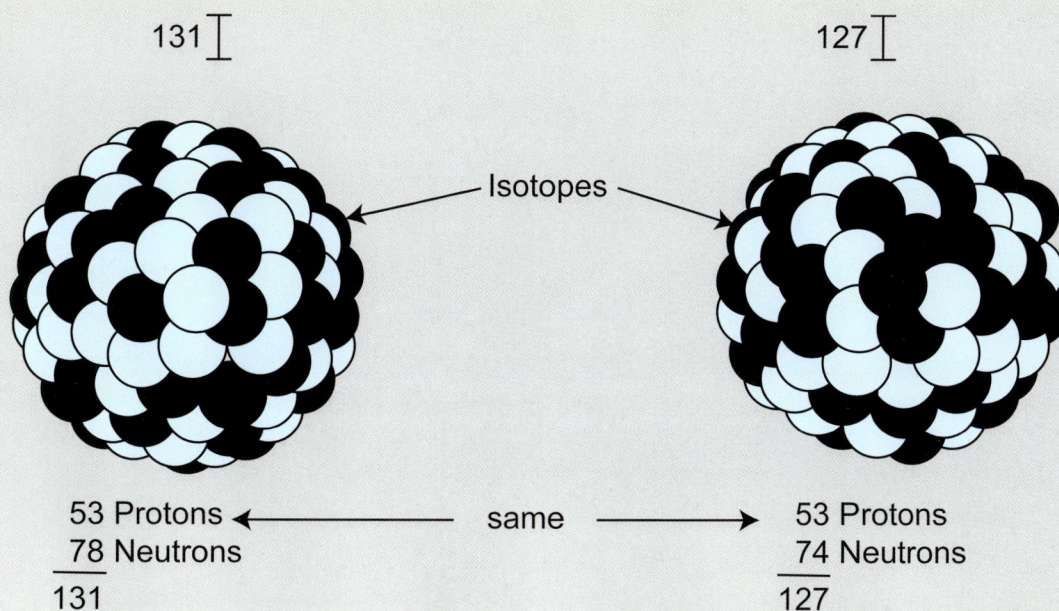

131		127
	Isotopes	
53 Protons	same	53 Protons
78 Neutrons		74 Neutrons
131		127

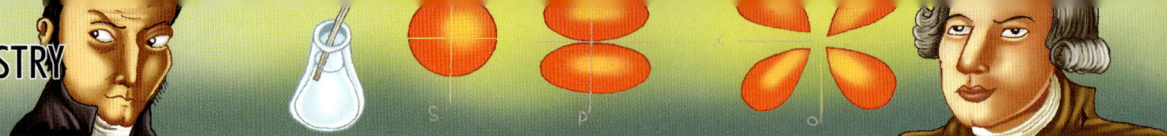

Orbitals and Quantum Numbers

Chemistry is mostly the study of electron interactions between atoms and molecules. Understanding the behaviour of the electrons in an atom is an important part of understanding chemical reactions. Electric attractive forces are much stronger than gravitational forces, but follow the same basic inverse square rules for distance. Early observations showed that electrons move more like a cloud surrounding the nucleus rather than an individual. The shape of the cloud, which

is now commonly known as orbital, depends on the amount of energy, angular momentum and magnetic moment of an electron. The properties of an atom's electron configuration are described by four **quantum numbers: n, l, m, and s.**

The first is the energy level quantum number, denoted by n. In an orbit, lower energy orbits are close to the source of attraction. Higher values of n mean more energy for the electron and the

	I A	II A										III A	IV A	V A	VI A	VII A	VIII A
Number of e- in Outer Shell (Group)																	
1	1s																1s
2	2s	2s										2p	2p	2p	2p	2p	2p
			III B	IV B	V B	VI B	VII B		VIII B		I B	II B						
3	3s	3s											3p	3p	3p	3p	3p	3p
4	4s	4s	3d	3d	3d	3d	3d	3d	3d	3d	3d	3d	4p	4p	4p	4p	4p	4p
5	5s	5s	4d	4d	4d	4d	4d	4d	4d	4d	4d	4d	5p	5p	5p	5p	5p	5p
6	6s	6s	5d	5d	5d	5d	5d	5d	5d	5d	5d	5d	6p	6p	6p	6p	6p	6p
7	7s	7s	6d	6d	6d	6d	6d	6d	6d	6d								

Shell Number (Period)

4f	4f	4f	4f	4f	4f	4f	4f	4f	4f	4f	4f	4f
5f	5f	5f	5f	5f	5f	5f	5f	5f	5f	5f	5f	5f

corresponding radius of the electron cloud or orbital is further away from the nucleus. Values of n start at 1 and go up by integer amounts. The higher the value of n, the closer the corresponding energy levels are to each other. If enough energy is added to the electron, it leaves the atom leaving behind a positive ion.

The second quantum number is the angular quantum number, represented by l. Each value of n has multiple values of l ranging in values from 0 to (n-1). This quantum number determines the 'shape' of the electron cloud. For l = 0, shape of electron cloud is called an 's' orbital. The second, l = 1 is called a p orbital. For l = 2, orbital is called a 'd' orbital. The next orbital as defined by l=3 is called an f orbital. So, there are four orbitals – s, p, d and f.

The third quantum number is the magnetic quantum number, m. These numbers were first discovered in spectroscopy when the gaseous elements were exposed to a magnetic field. The spectral line corresponding to a particular orbit would split into multiple lines when a magnetic field would be introduced across the gas. The number of split lines would be related to the angular quantum number. This relationship shows for every value of l, a corresponding set of values of m ranging from -l to l is found. This number determines the orbital's orientation in space. For example, p orbital corresponds to l = 1 and it can have m values of -1, 0, 1. This would represent three different orientations in space for the twin petals of the p orbital shape.

The fourth quantum number is the spin

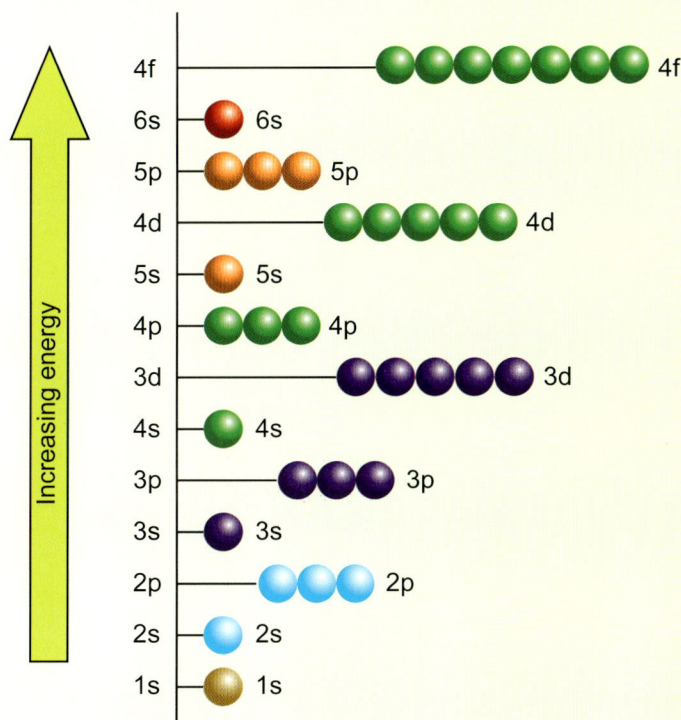

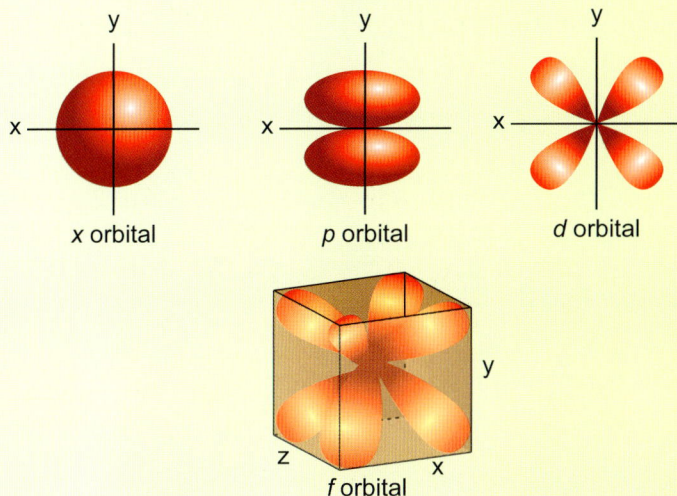

Orbitals

x orbital

p orbital

d orbital

f orbital

quantum number, s. There are only two values for s, +½ and -½. These are also known as 'spin up' and 'spin down'. This number is used to explain behaviour of individual electrons as if they were spinning in a clockwise or counter clockwise. The important part to orbital is the fact that each value of m has two electrons and needed a way to distinguish them from one another.

These four numbers, n, l, m and s can be used to describe any electron in a stable atom. Each electron's quantum numbers are unique and cannot be shared by another electron in that atom. A stable atom has as many electrons as it does protons.

Electronic Configuration: Filling of orbitals in atom

The distribution of electrons in different orbitals is known as electronic configuration of the atom. The orbitals are indicated by a square box and electrons are indicated by arrows. An empty square will mean an empty orbital, while a single electron will be indicated by drawing one arrow in the square and two electrons will be shown by a pair of arrows with their heads in the reverse direction. The direction of the arrow gives the orientation of its spin.

Alternatively, electronic configuration is expressed by indicating the principal quantum number and its respective

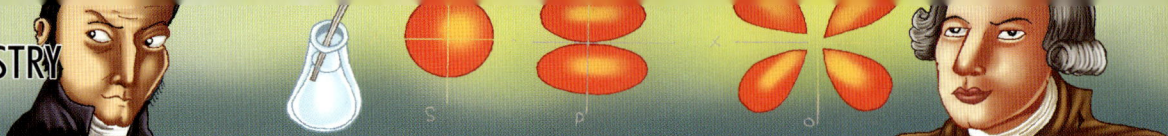

Nucleus

Electron Shells

orbital along with the number of electrons present in it. So, the way in which electrons are distributed among the various orbitals is called the electron configuration. The filling of electrons into the orbitals is governed by the following rules: Aufbau principle, Pauli's exclusion principle and Hund's rule of maximum multiplicity.

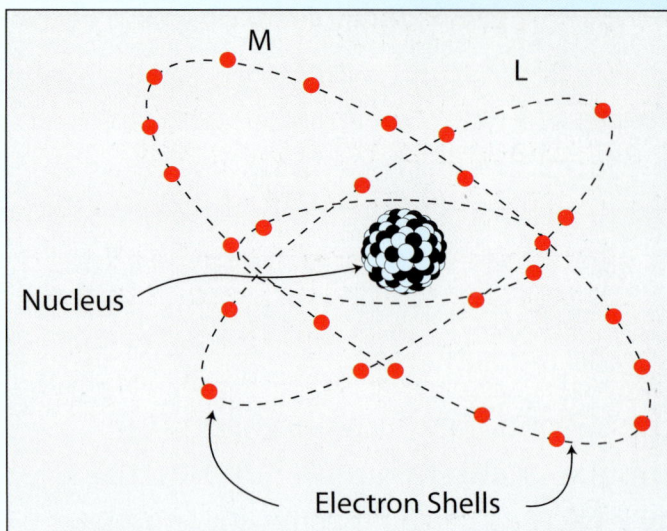

Aufbau Principle

The Aufbau principle states that in the ground state of an atom, an electron enters the orbital of lowest energy first, and then the subsequent electrons are fed in the order of increasing energies into the orbitals. The sequence of orbitals in the increasing energy is :1s, 2s, 2p, 3s, 3p, 4s, 3d, 4p, 5s, 4d, 5p, 6s, 4f, 5d, 6p, 7s.

According to Aufbau principle, the orbitals should be filled in the above sequence.

Pauli Exclusion Principle

This principle was proposed by Pauli in 1952. It states that no two electrons in an atom can have same values for all the four quantum numbers. Thus, in the same atom, two electrons may have the same values for three quantum numbers but the fourth must be different. Electrons having the same value of n, l and m are said to belong to the same orbital. So, the Pauli's exclusion principle may also be stated as 'An orbital can have maximum of two electrons and these two must have opposite spin'. The maximum number of electrons in each main energy level can be predicted by extending this principle.

Hund's Rule of Maximum Multiplicity

According to this rule, electron pairing will not take place in orbitals of same energy until each orbital is first singly filled with parallel spin. So, in a set of orbitals having same energy, the electrons distribute themselves to occupy separate orbitals with same spin as far as possible. This principle is very important in guiding the filling of p, d and f subshells, which have more than one type of orbitals.

Wolfgang Pauli was an Austrian physicist who was born on April 25, 1900 in Vienna, Austria. He discovered that each electron has its own unique quantum state. This is now known as the Pauli's Exclusion Principle. He was awarded 1945 Nobel Prize in Physics for his discovery.

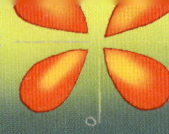

Some Nobel Prize winners for Chemistry

2010	Richard F. Heck, Ei-ichi Negishi, Akira Suzuki		1994	George A. Olah
2009	Venkatraman Ramakrishnan, Thomas A. Steitz, Ada E. Yonath		1993	Kary B. Mullis, Michael Smith
2008	Osamu Shimomura, Martin Chalfie, Roger Y. Tsien		1992	Rudolph A. Marcus
2007	Gerhard Ertl		1991	Richard R. Ernst
2006	Roger D. Kornberg		1981	Kenichi Fukui, Roald Hoffmann
2005	Yves Chauvin, Robert H. Grubbs, Richard R. Schrock		1980	Paul Berg, Walter Gilbert, Frederick Sanger
2004	Aaron Ciechanover, Avram Hershko, Irwin Rose		1979	Herbert C. Brown, Georg Wittig
2003	Peter Agre, Roderick MacKinnon		1961	Melvin Calvin
2002	John B. Fenn, Koichi Tanaka, Kurt Wüthrich		1958	Frederick Sanger
2001	William S. Knowles, Ryoji Noyori, K. Barry Sharpless		1954	Linus Carl Pauling
2000	Alan J. Heeger, Alan G. MacDiarmid, Hideki Shirakawa		1947	Sir Robert Robinson
1999	Ahmed H. Zewail		1938	Richard Kuhn
1998	Walter Kohn, John A. Pople		1935	Frédéric Joliot, Irène Joliot-Curie
1997	Paul D. Boyer, John E. Walker, Jens C. Skou		1930	Hans Fischer
1996	Robert F. Curl Jr., Sir Harold W. Kroto, Richard E. Smalley		1920	Walther Hermann Nernst
1995	Paul J. Crutzen, Mario J. Molina, F. Sherwood Rowland		1911	Marie Curie
			1909	Wilhelm Ostwald
			1908	Ernest Rutherford
			1903	Svante August Arrhenius
			1902	Hermann Emil Fischer
			1901	Jacobus Henricus van 't Hoff

Test Your MEMORY

1. What are the major branches of chemistry?

2. What do we study in Biochemistry?

3. Describe the SI system of units?

4. What is the difference between base units and derived units?

5. What are the laws of chemical combinations?

6. What is Avogadro number?

7. Write down the main postulates of Dalton's atomic theory?

8. Name the subatomic particles?

9. Define atomic number.

10. Explain quantum numbers.

11. What is empirical formula?

12. How do we fill electrons in orbitals of an atom?

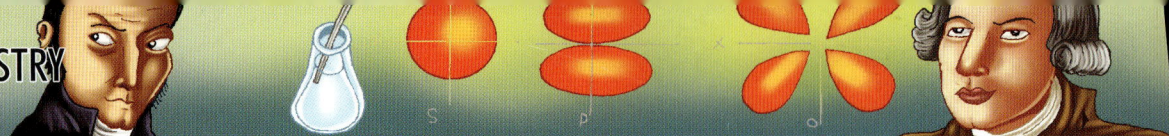

Index

A

Analytical Chemistry 6, 7
atomic mass 4, 19, 23, 25
atomic number 23, 25
atoms 3, 4, 5, 6, 14, 17, 18, 19, 20, 22, 23, 24, 25, 26
Avogadro Law 4, 17

B

Biochemistry 6, 7, 31

C

chemical educators 9
chemical kinetics 6

E

electron 19, 20, 26, 27, 28, 29, 30
electron configuration 26, 28, 29
Environmental chemists 9

F

Forensic chemists 9

G

Gay Lussac's Law of Gaseous Volumes 4, 16

I

industrial research chemists 9
Inorganic chemistry 5
International Bureau of Weights and Measures 10

International System of Units 3, 10
isotopes 4, 25
Isotopes, isobars and isotones 25

L

Law of Conservation of Mass 4, 13
Law of Definite Proportions 4, 14, 15
Law of Multiple Proportions 4, 14

N

neutron 19, 21
non-stoichiometric compounds 14
nucleus 19, 21, 22, 23, 26, 27

O

Organic chemistry 5

Q

quantitative analysis 7
Quantum Chemistry 6
quantum numbers 26, 28, 29, 30

S

sales representatives 9

T

The law of Reciprocal Proportions 15